KIDS' EDITION

TRAVEL LIKE AN ARCHITECT

The Basics

C. Evan H.

Disclaimer: This book is full of my thoughts and opinions which should not be taken as fact or law.

Paperback ISBN: 978-1-7377328-3-9
Ebook ISBN: 978-1-7377328-2-2

Library of Congress Control Number: 2021916482

First paperback edition August 2021

Edited by Kensi Bui
Illustrated by C. Evan H.
Cover art by C. Evan H.
Layout by C. Evan H.

Printed by Kindle Direct Publishing

Author Website: cevanh.myportfolio.com

TABLE OF CONTENTS

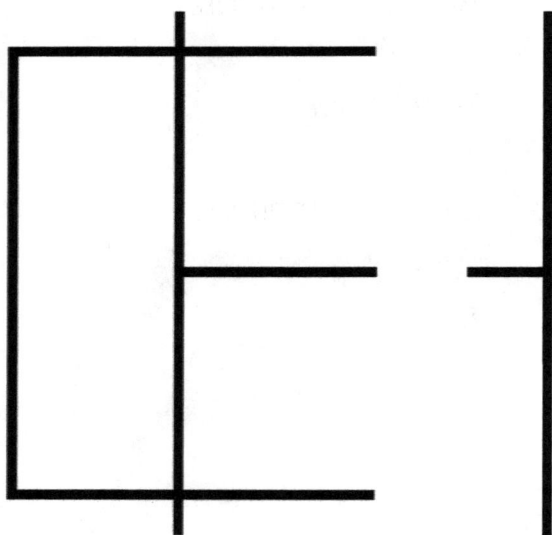

Hi, my name is C. Evan H., and I have a Master of Architecture degree.

What is architecture? Well, it's a fancy word for buildings like houses or grocery stores or sky-scrapers, but it could also sometimes mean parks or streets.

Because I love architecture, I also love to travel to see architecture.

Travel could mean a long trip with suitcases to another city, or it could mean a short walk around the neighborhood.

Architecture is a big part of travel since almost everywhere has buildings, so how do we enjoy it?

First, talk about how
the outside looks.

Then, talk about how
the inside looks.

The outside and the inside often look different, but every now and then the line is fuzzy.

Architecture can blend
in to its surroundings,
or it can stand out.

Some architecture is older than anyone on Earth, but other architecture is as new as a baby.

It may be easy to call some architecture ugly, but we shouldn't use the word ugly.

Everyone thinks different things are pretty, so nothing is really ugly. Everything has prettiness to somebody.

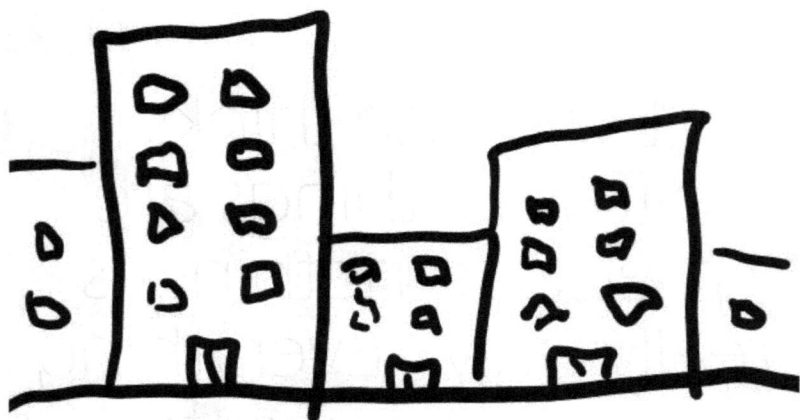

Another reason I like architecture is because it always has a story to why it was built.

These stories are "history", and mostly it's only known by a few people, but some architecture history is known by almost the whole world.

Sometimes architecture is filled with stories of brave heroes like the castles in Italy, and we can be loud and play.

9:01

Other times architecture tells sad stories like the Oklahoma City Bombing Memorial, and we need to be quiet and respectful.

History can be found in books, articles, videos, and movies. If we look closely, we can even see traces in the architecture itself!

Always remember
to ask grown-ups
questions about the
architectures' history

As interesting as architecture is, it's clear that it's something we must draw pictures of. Architects call these pictures "sketches."

BUILDING

DOOR

FOUNTAIN

And, when those sketches have words with them, we call them "Annotated Sketches."

Not all sketches are pretty, but all are fun to draw. Use the rest of this book for some architecture sketches.

ANNOTATED

SKETCHES

_____

_____

_____

_____

_____

ANNOTATED

_____

_____

_____

_____

_____

SKETCHES

_____

_____

_____

_____

_____

ANNOTATED

_____

_____

_____

_____

_____

SKETCHES

_____

_____

_____

_____

_____

ANNOTATED

_____

_____

_____

_____

_____

SKETCHES

_____

_____

_____

_____

_____

ANNOTATED

_____

_____

_____

_____

_____

SKETCHES

_____

_____

_____

_____

_____

ANNOTATED

_____

_____

_____

_____

_____

SKETCHES

_____

_____

_____

_____

_____

ANNOTATED

_____

_____

_____

_____

_____

SKETCHES

_____

_____

_____

_____

_____

ANNOTATED

_____

_____

_____

_____

_____

SKETCHES

WHERE WILL YOU
GO NOW?

KIDS' EDITION

TRAVEL LIKE AN ARCHITECT

GHOSTS OF SEGREGATION

C EVAN H

BE ON THE LOOK OUT

This is the first book in a series in which I will travel to different cities and comment on the aspect of architecture that interests me most: socio-political. For example, my next book will be titled "Travel Like an Architect: Ghosts of Segregation," and I will discuss how the segregation, red-line-ing, and gentrification of the black community can still be seen in the architecture of the Deep Deuce neighborhood in Oklahoma City. If that interests you, be sure to visit my website and subscribe to my newsletter to catch its release.

cevanh.myportfolio.com

C EVAN H

TRAVEL LIKE
AN ARCHITECT
THE BASICS

KNOW ANY GROWN-UPS? HAVE THEM CHECK OUT THE ORIGINAL EDITION OF THIS BOOK!

C EVAN H

ABOUT THE AUTHOR

C. Evan H. is a young graduate from the University of Oklahoma's Master of Architecture program. Though in his time there, he grew a passion for writing as much as he had for architecture. Like so many, he enjoys grabbing a cup of coffee and going on an adventure, whether that be across the world or to the grocery store. Learn more about him on his website:

cevanh.myportfolio.com

THANKS FOR READING!

Follow me on Instagram for updates on future books